Soul Musings

OTHER BOOKS BY THE AUTHOR:

Authentic Spirituality

Anatomy of Caring

A Caregiver's Journal

Soul Musings
Finding the Sacred in the Ordinary

CHRISTINE GREEN

Park Point
PRESS

Park Point Press | 573 Park Point Drive | Golden CO 80401

Soul Musings: Finding the Sacred in the Ordinary
Copyright © 2021, Christine Green

Park Point Press
573 Park Point Drive
Golden, CO 80401-7402
720-496-1370

www.csl.org/publications/books
www.scienceofmind.com/publish-your-book

Printed in the United States of America
Published September 2021

Editor: Julie Mierau, JM Wordsmith
Design/Layout: Maria Robinson, Designs On You, LLC

paperback ISBN: 978-0-917849-97-8
ebook ISBN: 978-1-956198-12-6

To Rev. Marjory Dawson,
my friend, my mentor, my muse

Table of Contents

Introduction

From as early as I can remember, I believed there just wasn't enough. Not enough time, not enough money, not enough resources. My belief served as a magnet, attracting situations of lack where opportunities seemed limited and resources were scarce. Growing up in upstate New York, I felt even the winter weather conspired to spoil my fun.

It wasn't until I embarked on my spiritual journey that I began to understand I had a choice. I could continue to believe that life was full of barriers and I was helpless, powerless, and couldn't have what I wanted, or I could choose to change my thinking and ultimately my belief.

I came to realize it's the little things that eat away at one's faith and conviction of good. If I am trapped in the turmoil of my daily upset and don't take the time to observe and reflect, I am at mercy to the conditions of the world. When I train myself to look beyond the circumstances, I discover my limiting beliefs and surrender their emotional grip on me. I then refocus and invite life-affirming declarations into my thinking. If I practice enough with the small daily irritations of the world, then I am not swayed when the big stuff happens. When I feel stuck or limited, I am the one who moved away from God.

The essays in *Soul Musings* were written before the 2020 COVID-19 pandemic, before life dramatically turned upside down. The uncertainty and chaos shook us to the core. The changing world will always present challenges and obstacles. But the spiritual truths remain the same. Spiritual principle is steadfast. Our opportunity is to stay in the practice, with gentleness and compassion for ourselves.

I am grateful to share my insights and revelations. When faith is applied, even the most ordinary life situations reveal wisdom and clarity. Opening to spiritual principle helps me remember God's love is always giving, blessing, and lifting me up even in the most difficult circumstances.

Soul Musings is a collection of stories, experiences, and insights that inspired and moved me. Each experience gave me the opportunity to see life in a new way, to find a nugget of spiritual insight that changed the way I looked at the world.

A musing is defined as a product of contemplation—a reflection, an inspiration. In our fast-paced world, sometimes it is important to stop and ponder the situations and experiences life presents to us. There is often a valuable revelation just waiting to be discovered.

My intention is that the insights and reflections in *Soul Musings* spark a fresh idea or provoke a question that shifts your thinking. Use the affirmations at the end of each essay to reframe limited thoughts. Use the journaling exercises to unearth buried dreams and inspire creative juices. Randomly select an essay as a morning practice to expand your spiritual awakening. Make the practices personal and feel free to replace the word God with Spirit, Universe, Source or whatever name you call the Divine.

Wherever you are on your journey, I honor your willingness to open your heart to the musings of your soul.

Soul Musings

Finding the Sacred in the Ordinary

You have permission to write in this book.
Let your creative process flow:

Write, draw, doodle, color,
scribble, sketch
your divinely inspired ideas.

It Does a Body Good

*"Only those who risk going too far
can possibly find out how far one can go."*

— T.S. Eliot

When I was around ten years old, my parents enrolled me in swimming classes at the new neighborhood pool. As I made progress, I was moved into the advanced group at the deep end of the pool. We lined up and, one by one, had to swim across. When it was my turn, I jumped in and swam half-way across the pool when I started to panic. I couldn't breathe and started flailing. The lifeguard dove in and brought me back to the side of the pool. Once I was OK, the instructor sent me back to the intermediate lessons. I felt embarrassed and ashamed.

I wish my instructor had taken the time to help me face whatever fear I was feeling and given me another chance to swim across the pool. Instead I felt like a failure and was punished and sent away.

We come face to face with our fears almost every day. All too often we quit and walk away, never knowing if we were going to reach our goal. Can we ever really fail? If we try something new and it doesn't work the way we want, we have the chance to reorganize and try again. Isn't that a kinder, gentler way to see it?

We build faith when we take risks and face fears. We discover resources and strengths we didn't know we had. We learn to trust that we have what we need when we need it.

There is freedom in faith. Faith is knowing that whatever is needed will be provided—whether it's having the strength to face a challenge, courage to speak the truth, or help in times of struggle.

Faith. It does a body good.

AFFIRMATION: I have strength to face any challenge, courage to speak my truth, and faith that whatever is needed is provided each day.

Journal Practice

What fears are you willing to face?

A Recipe for Faith

⁓⁓⁓

*"None of us knows what might happen even
the next minute. Yet still we go forward.
Because we trust. Because we have faith."*

— Paulo Coelho

Hang in there. Have you ever had a well-meaning friend share that bit of advice? How long should we *"hang in there?"* We wait for relationships to transform, for jobs to appear, for money to show up. Waiting comes from hope but is dampened by doubt.

Doubt is debilitating and disempowering. Doubt makes us afraid to take a step forward for fear of what might happen. What if I take the wrong action? What if things don't work out? Asking "what if" can sap our energy and leave us feeling ineffective. Years ago, I received a note in the mail with a card inside that said: *Dear Friend, I am working on all of your problems. Please stay out of the way. Love, God.* I was busy telling God what I wanted and how to get the job done. I prayed for help but never let go. I was willing—but I never surrendered.

No two people develop their faith the same way. I have found that the recipe for faith is one part willingness, two parts surrender, and three parts gratitude. Faith begins with a willingness to receive what we want without dictating the steps.

It is possible to take the steps needed without controlling the outcome. It's simple but not easy. Living in faith, we learn to live in gratitude for the process, the practice, and the patience.

AFFIRMATION:
I am open and receptive to all the good God has to offer.

Journal Practice

What are you willing to let go and let God handle?

Metamorphosis of Love

*"As the heart opens, it is drawn to pure freedom.
It replaces constant nitpicky control and management
of feelings with spontaneous originality
and profound inquiry, with love and devotion."*

— James O'Dea

Nothing can dismantle our plans for the day like a computer glitch. All activities come to a grinding halt. We can easily be catapulted into stress.

I got up from the computer and went for a walk in the garden. It was so soothing to see the blossoms on the trees, to smell the daphne, and admire the beautiful array of colors. Seeing and smelling nature allowed me to be centered again in love.

So many times during the day, we are sidetracked with challenges and problems, some belonging to us as well as to our friends and loved ones. We each have an opportunity to choose love instead of fear. Fear works like a stealth invader, activating alarms in the brain, stirring emotions into chaos, causing blood pressure to rise and the body to react. Whatever love we may have experienced quickly disappears.

It takes discipline and practice to stay centered to love. Feeling gratitude, remembering to breathe, whispering a prayer, listening to uplifting music, and connecting with beauty are just a few of the ways to inspire love.

Living in love brings us back to God.

AFFIRMATION: I am living in Love.

Journal Practice

What do you do to stay centered in love?

Liberate Your Thinking

_⟨⟩⟨⟩_

> "Most of our troubles are due to our passionate
> desire for and attachment to things
> that we misapprehend as enduring entities."
>
> — Dalai Lama

You may think it's strange, but I love to clean and organize things. Whether I organize my desk or clean out a closet, there is something therapeutic about letting go of clutter and bringing order. I feel liberated and have more clarity in my thinking.

Charles S. Fillmore said order is the first law of heaven. I think I know why. When we have order, we clear any confusion and chaos around us, and we experience more freedom and peace.

As I reorganized my garage, I boxed up old clothes, books, and some kitchen gadgets to give away. It felt so freeing to release and circulate those things I no longer need. I realized that we spend so much time declaring what we want, maybe it is just as important to identify old thoughts and beliefs we are ready to release.

I'm ready to let go of the belief that there is not enough time. I am willing to let go of the idea that getting older means having less energy. Letting go of old beliefs paves the way for innovative ideas, inspired plans, and new experiences to show up.

Faith plays an important part in letting go. When we live in faith, we trust that God guides and directs us on our journey. Faith is the spiritual assurance that whatever I need will be provided. Fillmore reminds us, "Faith is a deep inner knowing that that which is sought is already ours for the taking."

Letting go of unwanted belongings brings order, releasing old beliefs brings freedom, and living in faith brings peace. Knowing you are richly blessed with freedom, peace, and joy.

AFFIRMATION: I trust that I am guided and directed in all my activities.

Journal Practice

Make a list of beliefs you are willing to release and new beliefs you are willing to embrace.

Stepping Out in Faith

~⟨⟨⟨)⟩⟩~

*"Lighthouses don't go running
all over an island looking for boats to save;
they just stand there shining."*

— Anne Lamott

I love the scene in the movie *Indiana Jones and the Temple of Doom* where Harrison Ford's character stands at edge of the bottomless chasm while the bad guys are chasing him and coming closer. The chalice he is searching for is on the other side of the chasm, as is his freedom. He is at risk whether he stays or goes. Or so it seems. When he finally takes a step into the void, a step magically appears to support him. And another and another until he makes it to the other side.

That is the practice of faith. We walk out each day not knowing how or what will support each step we take and trust that what we need will show up. It is an individual process of growth, patience, and willingness. The practice yields ever-deepening faith and trust.

The presence of God is not limited to a church, a mosque, or a temple. We find God in our struggles and successes, in good days and bad.

We can have a mental understanding of what we think God is. But it is in the joy of a child's laughter, the beauty of a summer sunset, or the love of a friend's embrace that we are reminded of our connection with God that is love.

An important part of this work is the willingness to live in the void. To surrender. To acknowledge that I don't know what is next and I have no control over it. In that moment, I allow my human personality (ego) to fall away and let God step in. Now faith is the substance of things hoped for, the evidence of things not seen *(Hebrews 11:1).*

AFFIRMATION: I trust that all I need is revealed with ease and grace.

Journal Practice

Make a list of what are willing to surrender—and allow Spirit to show up.

The Power Is Love

⟨⟨⟩⟩

*"As you begin to think more about how you can
love your way through life, rather than about how you
have to battle your way through life, love
will reveal to you its secret success powers."*

— Catherine Ponder

A harsh word, a disapproving look, or an offhand comment from another can project us into feelings of unworthiness. Our sense of self-worth can feel diminished in an instant because of another's actions. The moment we relinquish our power to others, we feel both helpless and hopeless.

The need to be loved and accepted by others makes us vulnerable to feeling hurt, criticized, and judged. We tend to embrace these feelings as reflections of unworthiness. It is difficult to see beyond our own pain and distress to imagine the possibility of moving forward.

By consciously identifying victim thoughts and reframing them, we can begin to lift ourselves out of a victim mentality and reclaim our power. Wayne Dyer shares: "With everything that has happened to you, you can either feel sorry for yourself or treat what has happened as a gift.

"Everything is either an opportunity to grow or an obstacle to keep you from growing. You get to choose."

The power we ultimately search for cannot be found in the physical world. As we deepen in faith, we are empowered and allow Spirit to work through us. There is less attention on reassuring our ego and more appreciation for God expressing through us. The light of God within is the power we seek and that power is love.

The power of love heals, forgives, and makes new. Turning to our divine self instead of our victim self, we are powerful. We know our worthiness, and we live in harmony and freedom.

AFFIRMATION: I fully accept God's light and love in my life.

Journal Practice

Reframe your victim thoughts, using these examples.

Old: I can't do this.
New: I trust in Divine Wisdom to guide me.
Old: This will never work.
New: I am open to infinite possibilities.

Everyone Is Conspiring

～ﾉﾉ)))))～

*"Thoughts of condemnation, enmity, and resistance
must be released and divine love declared;
then faith will work unhindered."*

— Charles Fillmore

Past experiences about money stay with us for an inordinately long time. When I owned my first car, I needed to buy a new battery. I told my dad I was going to take my car to the garage in the neighborhood. "Oh no, don't do that," Dad declared. "He will take advantage of you and overcharge you." I asked him where he thought I should take my car. He ran through the list of car repair shops and dealers in the area. According to Dad, every one of them seemed to have nefarious business practices and could not be trusted. I was left feeling helpless and confused.

That feeling stayed with me for many years. I learned that I couldn't really trust people. I believed they were always out to trick or deceive me out of my hard-earned money.

It is wise to research and evaluate before we make decisions. But it is limiting and fearful to believe that no one is to be trusted. I've learned over the years to balance my thoughts and feelings. I do my best to look for the good in people. I affirm, "Everyone is conspiring to make me happy." Most people I meet are honest, trustworthy, and sincerely want to help.

Universal principle states: I receive what I believe. Seeing life through eyes of faith and love provides a much more uplifting experience.

I believe there is good for me and I deserve to have it.

AFFIRMATION: Everyone is conspiring to make me happy.

Journal Practice

Where are you willing to expand your trust?

No Regrets

*"When Jesus told us to love our enemies,
I suspect that he was talking about our inner enemies
too. He knew that love was
the only means by which to transform them."*

— Sue Monk Kidd

I was cleaning out some files and found a letter from a coworker from many years ago. I was manager of a project and she didn't like the way I handled a conflict. She identified the things I did wrong and what I said. She scolded me for not listening and not responding to the needs of others.

Now, my question is why did I save this letter? I have received stacks of notes, cards, and letters over the years thanking me for something I shared or taught and for how clients were inspired from my work with them.

Isn't that what we do? We remember the things gone wrong, the mistakes we made, and the people we hurt. We dwell on the negative, hoping we will never make that mistake again.

I learned so much from working with that project. I discovered a lot about myself and how to communicate with others. I realized the power that love and forgiveness play in every interaction. Marianne Williamson reminds us, "The practice of forgiveness is our most important contribution in our healing of the world."

The letter reminded me that making a mistake is only a regret if I didn't learn from it. Then it's time to let it go.

I forgave myself and the coworker who wrote the letter. I let go of the past as I shredded the letter and gave thanks for the reminder.

AFFIRMATION: I graciously let go of the past and appreciate the present.

Journal Practice

Make a list of past mistakes and what you learned. Then let them go.

Detour to Faith

⟋⟍⟍⟋⟍⟋

*"Knowing yourself deeply has nothing to do with
whatever ideas are floating around in your mind.
Knowing yourself is to be rooted in Being,
instead of being lost in your mind."*

— Eckhart Tolle

I was prepared for the New Year. I cleaned out the garage, organized my office, upgraded my computer, and was ready to take on the year.

There is a saying, *Life happens when we are making other plans.* Without warning, my husband, Laurence, developed blood clots in his hands that caused intense piercing pain. His doctors were puzzled as to the cause and worked diligently to ease the pain.

I had to pull on everything I have ever taught about faith. Now I was the student taking notes about life, faith, and prayer. Perspective of life changes so quickly. Things that would normally send me into a frenzy now seemed harmless. I developed great compassion for anyone with health issues or dealing with pain. I have a profound appreciation for the dozens and dozens of people who offered to pray.

In the past I would pray so bad things wouldn't happen: Please deliver me from evil. The truth is that life is messy—full of ups and downs, struggles and triumphs, pain and freedom. As much as I would like to keep it neat and tidy, life seems to have a mind of its own. What I know is that sometimes the uncomfortable and painful experiences are the ones that open the door to freedom.

Faith is the freedom in knowing that whatever I need will be provided, whether it's having the strength to face the day, courage to speak my truth, or help for a loved one. Faith is appreciating every day as a treasure and every experience as a gift.

"For I know the plans I have for you," declares the Lord, "plans to prosper you and not to harm you, plans to give you hope and a future." *(Jeremiah 29:11)*

AFFIRMATION: I know whatever I need will be provided and I am grateful for God's many blessings.

Journal Practice

List the areas where you can expand your faith.

Pierce the Fog

*"To meditate means to go home to yourself.
Then you know how to take care of the things that
are happening inside you, and you know how
to take care of the things that happen around you."*

— Thich Nhat Hanh

Life can feel so intense sometimes. We have instant news that is up close and personal, whether events happen in Iraq, Africa, or West Virginia.

Dealing with all of it can sometimes leave us feeling like we are moving through a fog: a little unclear what step to take next and most uncertain about what is on the other side.

The fog clouds the mind and creates confusion, low energy, high anxiety, and an inability to accomplish anything. The impulse is to shake off the fog as quickly as possible and get on with life. Don't stop, don't look back, move on ahead.

I recently found myself in such a frustrating state. I can't afford to be in a fog when I need to be working on my goals, checking off my to-do list, leaping over tall buildings with a single bound, and other such activities in my quest to serve the world.

I stopped where I was and took some time to meditate. By focusing on my breath instead of my thoughts, I felt more centered. With my mind at rest, I felt more peace in my body. As I felt peace in my body, I was open to possibilities. I eventually got back to my list and my life.

Taking the time to meditate connects us with our divinity. We don't have to do things alone, we can access the universal power that surrounds us and nurtures us.

It is the power that pierces the fog and guides our journey with grace.

Blessings for a clear and peaceful journey.

AFFIRMATION: I see through the fog and open myself to peace.

Journal Practice

Where are you willing to have more clarity?

With Ease and Grace

ϿϿϿ

"I could see peace instead of this."

— A Course in Miracles

I was having lunch with a friend recently when she said she did not like the entrée she ordered. I suggested she send it back and order something else, but she said she felt uncomfortable doing that. Instead she aimlessly poked at her food and complained while we tried to enjoy our time together.

I was disappointed that my friend's discomfort overshadowed our lunch. The incident reminded me of how many times I suffered through an experience, either afraid to ask for what I wanted or worried about what someone would think about me.

Why do we suffer? To suffer means to feel or endure pain. We suffer when we when we don't believe we can have what we want. We suffer when we resist change, when we're afraid of being judged, or when we worry needlessly. Whatever the reason, suffering causes us to fall into victim consciousness, feeling powerless and helpless.

I love the power of the Serenity Prayer: *God grant me the serenity to accept the things I cannot change, the courage to change the things I can, and the wisdom to know the difference.* There are times when we experience pain and suffering and cannot change the circumstances. We may not like our circumstances but we accept them and deal with them the best we can.

The greatest example of this was actor and activist Christopher Reeve. He accepted the limitation of his spinal cord injury but never let it defeat him. He changed what he could and led an extremely productive life. He used his circumstances to raise awareness about spinal cord injuries and to raise money for research for a cure.

Suffering is an option. It is a choice. When faced with a difficult experience in life, we can choose how we will deal with it. Here are three steps to take us out of the experience of suffering:

1. **Don't complain.** Complaining has a way of depleting all the energy out of life. When we complain, we put our attention on what is not working. So we see more of what is not working around us. If I say, "I don't have enough money," I continue to see all the places where there is not enough. Just for fun, practice not complaining for a day. Notice how you feel at the end of the day.

2. **Be open to possibilities.** Resist saying or thinking, "There's nothing I can do about this situation." Be willing to look at other options and avenues. Clara Barton spoke so passionately to this: "I have an almost complete disregard of precedent, and a faith in the possibility of something better. It irritates me to be told how things have always been done. I defy the tyranny of precedent. I go for anything new that might improve the past."

3. **Speak with intention.** Our words are powerful. Speak what you would like to have happen, rather than what you don't want. I add "with ease and grace" to the end of my statement of intention: "I will finish this project with ease and grace." "I will meet my deadline with ease and grace."

How we observe our experiences dictates whether we live in pain and suffering or freedom and power. Marianne Williamson says, "The attention we pay to the nature of our thinking is the most powerful attention we can pay. Our spiritual victory lies in rising above the mental forces of fear and limitation, using our awareness to purify our thought forms, thus attaining the power to heal and be healed."

AFFIRMATION: I am grateful that my mind is guided by wisdom and every activity accomplished with ease and grace.

Journal Practice

Where are you willing to let go of suffering?

Memory Upgrade

"Most of the most important things in the world have been accomplished by people who have kept on trying when there seemed to be no hope at all."

— Dale Carnegie

In the years before she passed, my mom had a number of health problems, dementia being one of them. At 11 a.m. she couldn't remember if someone gave her meds that morning; at 2 p.m. she couldn't remember if she had eaten lunch. One day she was upset with my sister because she hadn't been to visit her. My sister reminded her she spent the afternoon with her the day before. She surprised everyone one day when she remembered the name of the man who owned the little candy store in our neighborhood more than forty years ago. She remembered his children's names as well.

I was feeling sorry for Mom when I realized I have a similar short-term memory problem. I find myself stressing about a problem, wondering how it is going to work out. My short-term memory seems to falter when I fail to remember that I had a similar problem the week before that was easily resolved. It's easy to overlook how I've been supported and guided in life.

It's time for a memory upgrade. It is important to recognize and acknowledge the blessings we receive every day. Spiritual principle states that whatever we put our attention on increases. The more we acknowledge God's gifts, the more we open the door for more abundant blessings to show up.

AFFIRMATION: I am grateful for the guidance and support I receive every day.

Journal Practic

Make a list of any recent problems that were resolved.

Transforming Sales into Sharing

*"Mindfulness is about love and loving life.
When you cultivate this love, it gives you clarity
and compassion for life, and your actions
happen in accordance with that."*

— Jon Kabat-Zinn

My client was frustrated. She provides a valuable service and has an easy time meeting people. She was stuck when it came time to telling them about her business. She didn't want to be a pushy salesperson.

The word "salesperson" is so outdated. I know very few salespeople. The guy who sold me my car was one. The telemarketer who tried unsuccessfully to sell me a vacation in Las Vegas was another. They weren't interested in me; they wanted me to buy what they were selling.

I shared with my client that perhaps she didn't need to sell anything. She has been in her industry for twenty years, has a wealth of information, and a list of successful clients. Her job is to get to know people and what they are interested in. The more engaged we are in others, the more engaging we are to others. The power is in building relationships. Businesses become successful because of our relationships and how much we care for each other.

I watched a friend build his successful business from the ground up. I noticed how he paid attention to people and remembered facts about their families and interests. He sincerely wanted to see others succeed. In return, he excelled and prospered in his work.

Our practice is to spend more time giving rather than receiving, sharing rather than withholding, lifting up rather than pressing down, and developing the earnest desire to see others to succeed. What you give out in love returns multiplied abundantly.

AFFIRMATION: I engage with others in love.

Journal Practice

Make a list of the ways you give in love.

Are You Listening?

〜〉〉〉〉〉〉〜

*"Too often we underestimate the power of a touch,
a smile, a kind word, a listening ear, an honest
compliment, or the smallest act of caring, all of which
have the potential to turn a life around."*

— Leo Buscaglia

I arrived at the bank with the necessary paperwork in my bag and courage in my heart. Even though Laurence had been gone for more than a month, his checking account made it feel like he was still present. Closing the account felt like I was closing off another part of his life. Another part of him was disappearing.

The teller directed me to a bank associate sitting at a desk. Choking back tears, I whispered I was there because my husband passed away and I needed to close his account. He examined the paperwork and clicked away on this computer keyboard. "So what are you doing to enjoy this sunny afternoon?" he asked mindlessly.

Seriously? I just handed you my husband's death certificate and you are asking me if I am enjoying the sunshine? If he had acknowledged my pain, perhaps he wouldn't have seemed so rude. Maybe I wouldn't have felt offended if he said, "I am so sorry for your loss. Let me see what I could do."

I don't know how long I stared at him, first stunned by his insensitivity and then editing the litany of comments I would have liked to shout at him. God was watching over me because before I could answer, he was called away to handle another question.

It takes patience to manage grief. Most of the time, I find compassion when I hear hurtful things and know it's not intentional.

I hope I am never so distracted that I am not aware of

what someone is feeling. In that moment, I made a vow to listen with more empathy. I asked God to guide me to speak words to others that are uplifting. I ask daily for the strength to learn how to forgive.

AFFIRMATION: I am guided to speak and listen with love.

Journal Practice

Acknowledge any loss or grief you are experiencing. Writing about it helps you release it.

Love Is Always the Answer

~⟫⟫〉⟫~

"Courage is what it takes to stand up and speak;
courage is also what it takes to sit down and listen."

— Winston Churchill

A friend shared with me that she was laid off from her job. Losing her job after so many years was painful. What added to the stress was that no one at the office acknowledged she was leaving. She felt invisible. She was not looking forward to returning for her last day.

I emailed suggestions about how to approach her office mates and leave with her head held high. I felt so good that I was able to help her.

I later realized I was giving her unsolicited advice, although she graciously received it. I noticed that I was reacting to my own pain of how debilitating and helpless that feeling of being invisible can be. I responded with my plan of how I would handle the situation—if it were me.

I Imagine what my friend wanted more than anything was for someone to listen and to have compassion for her pain and her loss.

Listening is a powerful gift. In that moment of listening, we pause and take a breath to really hear what is being shared. I know I respond best when I know the other person is paying attention and not trying to fix me.

Years ago, a job transfer took me to a new city where I didn't know anyone and felt isolated and overwhelmed. I called to talk with my mom about it. Her reply was, "Why don't you just quit and come home. You don't need to put up with all that." Yikes! I jumped up from my cowering fetal position. I didn't want to quit and I definitely did not want to go home. This new city was my home. I was simply venting and complaining. Her comment startled me enough to stop whining and get on with my life.

The urge to help others is noble but sometimes premature. If we listen long enough, the speaker discovers their own answer or the right question to ask. Listening allows us to move from helping to a place of service.

Being in service, we have no attachment to the right answer or the best solution, only an opportunity to listen in love.

And isn't love always the answer?

AFFIRMATION: I am willing to listen and to be of service.

Journal Practice

How do you practice listening?

Melting Away Beliefs

꧁꧂

*"When we experience our own desire for transformation,
we are feeling the universe evolving through us."*

— Barbara Marx Hubbard

I have a lot of compassion when I talk with potential clients. I hear how they have worked on their issues, tackled their problems, and confronted their pain: *I dealt with that problem when I was in rehab. I did a lot of processing when my relationship ended. I worked on that issue three years ago when I lived in Kansas.*

They are so ready to be finished with the pain and discomfort and ready to move on with life. Why does the same problem resurface again and again?

Working on deep-seated issues is not a one-time attempt. A belief can be compared to an iceberg. There are emotions and fears on the surface. We face them and they seem to go away for awhile, but we are astonished when they show up again. The healing work we do is the tip of the iceberg. Just as the sun melts away the ice on the surface, we are able to melt away the beliefs and fears that show up.

However, just like an iceberg, there is much more below the surface than we are aware of. The beliefs that cause us pain were rooted in us long ago and have had years to build and solidify. It seems like the problems never go away. Rev. Lloyd Strom states, "It often takes time, combined with daily dedicated spiritual practice, to completely dissolve a major belief in the sea of our soul."

Spiritual practice is not a mystery. It is the time that we spend contemplating, forgiving, praying, and feeling grateful. As we spend time devoted on what is going on inside, we begin to melt away the pain on the outside. The faith we build through spiritual practice helps us face our fears and confront our challenges, while knowing our needs are provided for.

AFFIRMATION: I have the patience and willingness to do my inner work.

Journal Practice

What do you do for your daily spiritual practice?

The Voice

〜〜〜

*"It's not easy to subdue the overweening ego
in order to free the adventuresome soul.
But whenever we manage to do so,
it saves us grief and serves the world well."*

— Parker Palmer

Have you listened to the voice lately? No, not the TV show with the amazing singers. I mean the voice in the back of your mind. Some days it reminds me of being in a car with a backseat driver who is constantly nagging, criticizing, and listing all the things I've done wrong. It can be exhausting!

The inner critic is sneaky. It shifts attention away from itself and makes us believe that "those people" are the enemy. THEY are the ones judging and criticizing us. THEY are the ones keeping us from success. THEY are the ones who are out to make life miserable for us.

Truth is, there is only us. THEY are a fabrication of our imagination. THEY are not separate from us, they ARE us. We are all in this journey of life together. THEY were created out of fear. Together we are love.

When I step out from behind the walls and barricades, I look out at the smiling faces of people who are glad to see me. I notice people who are eager to help and those who are willing to listen. They have been there all along. I've been too afraid to notice.

The next time the voice in the backseat starts ranting about what you are doing and where you are going, tell it to chill, be quiet, or take a hike.

There is no time to listen. Life is full of connecting and collaborating with others. We are on a mission to make the world a better place for all of us.

AFFIRMATION: I walk out each day in faith and joy.

Journal Practice

What are some of the false beliefs you hear from your inner critic? What do you want instead?

Illusion of Separation

*"Forgiveness is not always easy.
At times, it feels more painful than the wound
we suffered, to forgive the one
that inflicted it. And yet,
there is no peace without forgiveness."*

— Marianne Williamson

Have you ever held a grudge against someone? I did and noticed it was keeping me pretty occupied. Avoiding them, trying not to think about them, trying hard to pretend they didn't hurt me ... it was exhausting.

When we don't forgive, we stay in the struggle. We are in bondage with anger, bitterness, and resentment. When we don't forgive, we find there is a wall that separates us from love and keeps us from moving forward.

Forgiveness is an opportunity to let go. Forgiveness puts an end to the illusion of separation. It takes courage to let go—and when we do, it is one of the most important processes that brings harmony to our life and peace to our soul. Forgiveness sets us free to express love into the world.

Ernest Holmes states in *This Thing Called You,* "It may seem strange that the law which now holds you in bondage can as easily give you freedom. But this is the truth."

AFFIRMATION: I am willing to forgive and allow love to be expressed in the world.

Journal Practice

Who are you willing to forgive?

Anti-Grief Formula

"Grief can be the garden of compassion.
If you keep your heart open through everything,
your pain can become your greatest
ally in your life's search for love and wisdom."

— Rumi

A month after Laurence passed, I went to a department store at the mall and headed to the cosmetics counter. I purchased a bag of moisturizers, serums, and lotions, all promising anti-wrinkle, anti-aging, anti-sagging.

I didn't know how to say it but I was really looking for an anti-grief formula. I wanted a product that would magically erase my grey, sagging, sad-looking outlook. Something that would bring back the sparkle I had when I looked at Laurence. Something that would make me smile the way he smiled at me. I wanted a product that would make me excited and hopeful again.

Problem is, this is an inside job.

I learned I needed to love myself and have compassion for my life. I was willing to work through the pain and see the blessings along the way.

AFFIRMATION: I love and accept myself, just as I am.

Journal Practice

Identify any areas of life where you are grieving and give thanks for them.

Unexpected Blessings

꒰ ꒱

*"Grace is a mystical substance,
not a mental concept. As a mystical substance,
it must be experienced to be known."*

— Carolyn Myss

It was a snowy, frigid March day in upstate New York and my sister was working from home. She looked out her window late in the afternoon and saw snow piled high on the back deck. She headed to the garage to retrieve the snow blower. When she got to the driveway she stopped in amazement. The long driveway had already been plowed. Completely. Even the area around the mailbox. She called the next-door neighbors and friends down the road to see who performed such a gracious deed.

Everyone was busy with their own driveways. No one had stopped to clean hers.

Grace. Good will. Favor. Unexpected blessing. Charles Fillmore declares, "By becoming receptive to the 'Grace of God,' we receive the measure of God's provision, which exceeds any of our imaginings."

The human mind is bound by time, space, and conditions. But as we deepen in our realization of Spirit, we move into another dimension of being. As we look beyond the appearances of the world, we recognize that there is something more powerful, more expansive than what our limited imaginations can perceive.

Staying connected to our spiritual practice and continuing to build faith opens us to the amazing blessings of God's love. Grace isn't a mystery. It is available to us at every moment. Our willingness allows us to be receptive to possibilities.

AFFIRMATION: I am open and receptive to infinite possibilities.

Journal Practice

List your unexpected blessings.

The Wheels of Life

"Sometimes we can't get what we want. While this can be disappointing and painful, it is only devastating if we stop there. The world thrives on endless possibilities."

— Mark Nepo

One day I noticed one of the tires on my car looked a little flat. I stopped at the gas station to put air into it. The tire was not inflating, no matter how much air flowed into it. After a visit to the tire store, I found out the tire had a bad valve.

The car manual states that inflating car tires with the correct amount of air is essential for maximizing gas mileage and ensuring even tire wear. The same goes for maintaining the balance of spirit, mind, and body. If we sustain a constant relationship with our spiritual practice (meditation, journaling, prayer, spiritual mentoring, etc.), we are able to retain a peaceful mind and ease in our daily activities.

Do you ever have one of those days when it feels like you're moving through cement trying to get something done? That's a good indication of being out of spiritual balance. Our once peaceful experience leaks out and the body feels deflated and lacks energy. Getting anything accomplished feels like mission impossible. Stress builds in the body and doubt creeps into the mind.

Doubt can show up like a bad valve in our thinking. No matter how many positive affirmations, prayers, or good thoughts we have in the moment, doubt is a slow leak that can leave us drained, diminished, and discouraged.

Tire pressure is measured in PSI or pounds per square inch. Spiritual balance can be measured in DDP or daily dedicated practice. As we maintain our practice, we leave little room for doubt or uncertainty to take hold.

The flat tire reminded me that while traveling the often rough, bumpy road of life, it is important to take the time to maintain spiritual balance. It can boost our faith and keep the wheels of life moving with ease and grace.

AFFIRMATION: I gratefully travel along the road of life with ease and grace.

Journal Practice

Identify some places where you are spiritually out of balance. What do you want instead?

Empowered Ideas

✧⁓⁓✧

"It's kind of fun to do the impossible."

— Walt Disney

Ideas are like unlimited points of energy floating around the universe that we can't see or feel. All too often, we have an idea and we simply watch it float by. When our mental atmosphere is filled with "I can't," "I don't have time," or "I don't know what to do," there is no place for the idea to latch onto and stick. Have you ever had an idea and neglected to take action only to watch someone else grab onto it and run with it, resulting in overwhelming success? Wish I had thought of that....

Inspiration is defined as the result of an inspired activity, an idea. When we have developed the discipline to stay connected to our spiritual awareness, we open ourselves to infinite potential and allow our ideas to take shape. Discipline helps us overcome the mental blocks that stop the ideas from taking hold.

When we have the discipline to train our minds and take action to empower the ideas, we can achieve results that excite, motivate, and inspire us. When we use our ideas for the good of humanity, we receive rewards we cannot even begin to imagine.

AFFIRMATION: I am grateful for my divinely inspired ideas.

Journal Practice

Today, right now, make a list of your ideas.
Put a star next to the one you want to work on first.

Olympic Gold

⟋⟍⟍⟋⟍

*"Faith is taking the first step
even when you don't see the whole staircase."*

— Dr. Martin Luther King Jr.

I was in awe watching Olympic athletes compete and their commitment to train day after day, week after week, year after year. I was amazed by their persistence to keep going no matter what obstacles came their way. I respected their courage to continue even though they had injuries, surgeries, and life challenges.

I imagine they have fears and doubts just like the rest of us. What keeps them motivated is the vision of what is possible. They have the faith to keep moving forward, no matter what happens. When I listened to them being interviewed, they were ecstatic about how much they loved their sport.

Ultimately, love is our highest vision. Whether we want to accomplish something in the world or envision something greater for our families, the desire in our hearts is to express love.

Accomplishing our goals can be compared to climbing a mountain. The exquisite experience of joy is the end result. Faith is the fuel that keeps us climbing. Love is the inspiration that keeps us moving. Forgiveness melts any obstacle in our way, while gratitude infuses us with oxygen to keep us going.

Faith is an individual process of growth, patience, and willingness. As we let go of the pictures of doubt and replace them with a vision of love, we can reach any mountaintop. Faith is the real Olympic gold.

AFFIRMATION: I am motivated by love and inspired by faith.

Journal Practice

What goals do you want to achieve?

I Could See Peace

> *"Having an open mind and an open heart opens the*
> *door to love. But this is a door that opens and closes.*
> *When it closes, one needs to be patient*
> *and forgiving, or the door will not open again."*

— Paul Ferrini

I like to think of myself as a positive person. Most of the time, I do my best to find the highest thought in any situation. One day I noticed that as I witnessed someone with negative energy and anger, my tendency was to run in the opposite direction. It occurred to me that there may be a powerful healing opportunity if I could just stand still and not flee.

Since our human nature is 98 percent emotional and 2 percent rational, conflict causes a physical feeling of anxiety and an emotional feeling of insecurity. When we experience anxiety, we have a choice between reacting or reflecting. When we neglect to choose, our default mode is reactive.

Our reactive mode runs the gambit: Do we fight or flee, struggle or surrender, attack or withdraw? The need to appease is part of the reactive mode. All too often we suppress or deny our true feelings in order to appease. We can change this pattern by speaking our truth using "I" statements instead of "you" statements.

There is a lesson in *A Course in Miracles* that invites us to focus our thinking: "Peace of mind is clearly an internal matter. It must begin with your own thoughts, and then extend outward. It is from your peace of mind that a peaceful perception of the world arises." The lesson invites us to notice our fearful, anxiety-producing thoughts and offending behaviors or events and repeat a new thought: *I could see peace instead of this.*

By choosing to see peace, we have an opportunity to observe and relate to the situation at hand in a new way. We may still be troubled by the conflict and yet observe it with an intention for clarity. The practice engages our spiritual nature and guides us to a more peaceful solution.

Mother Theresa said, "If we really want to love, we must learn how to forgive." We can learn to forgive when we are willing to reflect and not react. Forgiveness takes humility, practice, and commitment. It changes our experience of the world to one of peace.

AFFIRMATION: I live in the moment. I live in love.

Journal Practice

When do you feel fear and want to run the other way?

Can You Hear Me Now?

⚒

"You cannot truly listen to anyone
and do anything else at the same time."

— M. Scott Peck

Hello? Anyone there? Are you listening? Very often we think we are listening but our mind is wandering off to other topics. This is prevalent today as we engage in multi-tasking in an unhealthy way. We may be on the phone with someone, while we are also responding to emails, reading mail, preparing dinner, or engaging in any number of other tasks. It is rare to have a one-to-one conversation anymore without also addressing other tasks. We lose sight of the divinity of the other person when we listen in this way.

Other times we think we are listening but we are so reactive to what the person is saying that we are busy formulating a reply and not really listening to what they are saying at all. We're cheating the person speaking out of truly hearing what they have to say.

The true gift of listening happens when we are fully present and receptive to what another person is saying. We may not fully agree with what they are saying, but we honor and listen to their story.

Words of wisdom from Fred Rogers, host of *Mr. Roger's Neighborhood,* a popular children's TV program: "The greatest gift that you can give another person is to gracefully receive whatever it is that they want to give us."

Notice the next time you are talking with someone. Are they fully present? What does that feel like? Now think about what it would take to be fully present for someone else. That would be an awesome gift.

AFFIRMATION: I am willing to be fully present and listen attentively.

Journal Practice

Make a list of ways you can listen more consciously.

A Gift of Love

꧁꧂

*"Every one of us needs to show how much
we care for each other and,
in the process, care for ourselves."*

— Princess Diana

I was sitting at a coffee shop one day and overheard two women talking. One of them declared that she would never again marry someone who was sick. She didn't want to endure the pain and responsibility.

I was struck by her comment. As demanding and difficult as the past years were, I would do it all again. The opportunity to care for my husband changed me. It opened my heart wider, deepened my faith, and showed me how much I was loved.

I learned how to receive all that my remarkable husband had to give to me. I discovered how to accept love, compassion, and any acts of gracious kindness from our friends and family. I awakened to gathering in God's amazing grace. I realized the extraordinary power of prayer.

While the tide of grief ebbs and flows in my life, I have stepped into a new awareness of courage and strength. Though I truly miss the opportunity to hug and hold my beloved, I feel his presence watching over me. I hear his whispers of comfort and answers to my questions. I feel his love enveloping me and empowering me.

As I noted in *Anatomy of Caring*, "Caregiving is not for the tender-hearted. It is a ministry of service. Seen as anything other than that it becomes a chore, a struggle, and burnout is sure to follow. Caregiving calls each of us to give of our time, energy, and stand face to face with fears and limitations. It is a test of faith. Above all, it is a gift of love."

AFFIRMATION: I know that as I give, my good is returned to me multiplied.

Journal Practice

List some times in your life when you faced fears and limitations.

Imagine the Possibilities

"Whatever I choose to believe becomes true for me."

— Louise L. Hay

Accusation, blame, and criticism—these are what I call the ABCs of complaining. It takes our attention off our own doubt and places it onto others. After all, isn't it our friends and family members who cause the problems? If they would just get in, get out, get going we would be alright. Honestly, the problem is that complaining zaps the energy right out of us.

If we believe our words have power, then using them to complain is to keep our problems alive. Instead of choosing words of faith or love, complaining keeps us trapped in the old pattern of thinking and keeps us reliving in the past. The Law of Attraction works both ways: Whatever you put your attention on increases. When we focus on what is not working, our energy, enthusiasm, vitality, and passion begin to spiral down and leave us listless and lifeless.

What do I want instead? This is an important question that takes us out of the downward spiral and lifts us up into the realm of possibility.

Possibilities activate our imagination, causing us to look upward and beyond the current experience. Opening to imagination opens us to the limitless expression of Spirit.

Imagining the potential of a life of harmony, peace, and prosperity changes the energy down to the very cells of our bodies. More importantly, we have the power to imagine what we want. Each one of us has the ability to transform doubt into faith.

There is no longer room for doubt in your consciousness. There is no longer room for doubt in your experience of life. You have the faith to live life fully and with joy.

AFFIRMATION: I release any belief in doubt and I live with faith and joy.

Journal Practice

What do you really want?

Only the Lonely

I understand loneliness. I have felt extremely alone in a crowded room. Making myself invisible would have been a blessing. Instead the loneliness creeps in as I awkwardly try to fit in. There are times I work hard at pretending to be an extrovert, while my introvert tendencies want me to get up and run as fast as my legs will carry me.

We don't prepare ourselves for loneliness. Life is busy. Demands are intense. Suddenly and without warning, we find ourselves alone. There are people around but they are busy. Too hurried to stop. Too overwhelmed to take the time to talk.

I have yet to find a solution. Faith helps my mind understand but doesn't always heal the hole in my heart.

We move through life one day at a time. Notice the sunset. Feel grateful. Find something that will bring a smile. Give thanks for the opportunities to love. Reach out to someone else who is feeling alone.

I was talking with a friend recently and she said the most important thing she looked for in a relationship was someone who got who she was, someone who understood her and accepted her quirky habits. Being accepted, being understood is a big part of being loved.

I know I am part of a universal presence of good. I know I am loved in spite of my loneliness.

You are loved. Right where you are, you are loved.

AFFIRMATION: I am loved unconditionally.

Journal Practice

What do you do to remember you are loved?

This, Too, Shall Pass

*"When we are no longer able to change
a situation—we are challenged
to change ourselves."*

— Viktor E. Frankl

Feel any emotions lately? I sure have. All of them. Sometimes all at once. It can feel like riding Doctor Doom's Fear Fall at Universal Orlando Island of Adventure over and over again. Hang on!

The adrenaline from emotional reaction is intoxicating. As stressful as the events of the world may seem, they are so much more entertaining than our own day-to-day issues. It can be addictive. Until we crash and burn.

Most people have little awareness about what is in their subconscious nature until it reaches the senses as emotion. Emotions give us signals about what we believe. If I feel threatened by an event happening in the world, my emotions flare up. The event didn't cause my emotions. What I believe about the event is the true source of my turmoil.

In an effort to get off my own roller coaster of emotions, I have returned to my mindfulness practice. Mindfulness is a technique that keeps me focused on the present moment. I am aware of my thoughts but resist the immediate need to act on them.

Then I stop, breathe, and center. I can still take action but I am choosing from a centered awareness rather than an impulse to react.

Stop. Breathe. Center. Know that this, too, shall pass.

AFFIRMATION: I am not the victim of the world I see.
There is another way of looking at the world. I could see
peace instead of this.

— A Course in Miracles

Journal Practice

What emotions are stirred up in you? Make a list.
Breathe and release.

Who Cares?

"It is well to say that God is unbounded, unlimited Love. God is our love. There is an instinctive seeking of all things for love. Love is another name for life."

— Emma Curtis Hopkins

I was born into a family of caregivers. My dad was one of the oldest of twelve children and he left high school to get a job so he could help support his family. In the 1960s, my grandfather suffered a number of strokes and was unable to walk. He weighed more than 200 pounds and my grandmother wasn't strong enough to move him. For ten years, my mother went to their home every night and put my grandfather to bed. And each morning she got him up and dressed and sat him in his chair.

My sister cared for my dad, who lived at home alone, and my mom, who lived in a nursing home for several years. I cared for my husband through his surgeries and illness.

I could list endless stories of family and friends who care for each other in time of need. I'm sure you have a list of your own caregivers.

Caregiving is complex. It demands that we be patient, strong, persistent, fearless, and gentle. We are called on to be advocates, listeners, errand-runners, and negotiators. At the same time, we deal with our own feelings of guilt, failure, disappointment, and fear. All while trying to take care of ourselves so we can care for others.

And yet in the midst of pain, fear, and sorrow, the opportunity to be a caregiver is truly a gift. The time we spend with our loved ones is precious. There is an awareness of love that is amazingly profound. We experience an extraordinary deepening of faith.

Who cares? I do. And I know you do, too. We care

because we love and we love because we care.

I absolutely know that God cares for us and loves us unconditionally. And just when we think we can't face another day, God sends us a caregiver to give us a call or a hug or lend a helping hand. "What no eye has seen, what no ear has heard, and what no human mind has conceived the things God has prepared for those who love him." *1 Corinthians 2:9 NIV*

AFFIRMATION: I am love and give love unconditionally.

Journal Practice

What are you willing to ask for?

Ordinary Into Extraordinary

∽∭∬∾

"Where there is love there is life."

— Mahatma Gandhi

I learned over the years that it was more important to create my own happiness than expect it to come from someone else. No one can fill the feelings of emptiness, loneliness, and lack. I have to find happiness within myself.

I know I cannot feel love when I have feelings of resentment, separation, and blame. I've trained myself to take a gratitude walk. I get out of the house and walk through the neighborhood or nearby park and take notice of the beauty and abundance around me. The walk always brings me back to God.

We must be love to find love. When we feel love, we appreciate the preciousness of life and all that life has to offer. When we are in a state of appreciation, we have a greater realization of our connection with God, can see the bigger picture of life, and that moves us into a greater experience of love.

Love transforms ordinary moments into extraordinary opportunities. Loving someone without wanting or needing anything is the greatest gift we can give. Loving and accepting someone unconditionally is like sending positive ions or invisible vitamins to them.

Love blesses the giver and the receiver.

If I listen to someone's story, make someone smile, or perform a random act of kindness, I've sent love to that person. When they feel love, they will share it with someone in their circle of influence. The experience has a ripple effect, like a stone being tossed in the water. Not only have I sent love to another person, I have expanded the experience for myself.

Love is an inside job. It starts with letting go of the pain from the past. As we acknowledge and appreciate others, we begin to receive it ourselves.

And it is contagious.

AFFIRMATION: I am open to receive the extraordinary moments of love.

Journal Practice

Make a list of what you appreciate about your life.

The Tribe Has Spoken

*"To see ourselves clearly, with eyes wide open,
we must learn to face ourselves objectively
and unsentimentally, denying nothing and being
willing to meet each new layer of the psyche
as it progressively reveals itself to us."*

— Mariana Caplan

Have you ever noticed that the moment you decide to take action toward a goal, your internal tribe members show up? So similar to the contestants on the *Survivor* reality show, they are extremely manipulative in churning up doubt, fear, and criticism. Now an all-out battle rages between the enthusiasm of your goal and the emotions of doubt.

Doubt is a fabrication of our imagination. As imagination fuels doubt, we begin to notice more and more limitation confronting us. As we imagine the effects of doubt, it becomes our reality, a truly vicious and nasty cycle.

Imagine what life would be like if doubt had stopped the inventor of the light bulb, the radio, or (gasp!) the internet. How many times a day do we squash an idea because we don't know how to put it into action or fear what other people think?

Those inner tribe members can be nasty, judgmental, disparaging and they sabotage our chances to succeed. Use the power of your imagination and vote them out of your thinking. They have no place and no power over you. Banish them and replace them with faith.

As you substitute the negativity of doubt with images of what you want, you become inspired about how you would like to express your talents in the world. Focus on your faith. Faith is an individual process of growth, patience, and willingness. Faith gives us the courage to speak the truth and the strength to face the day.

In his book *Conscious Union with God,* Joel Goldsmith states, "Regardless of the particular activity in which you are engaged, contact God within yourself and trust that contact to bring to you all that is necessary for your unfoldment."

You are the tribal council. You have the power. Vote doubt out off the island and out of your thinking.

The tribe has spoken.

AFFIRMATION: I am empowered and I take action with clarity and wisdom.

Journal Practice

Make a list of doubts you are willing to release.

It's Not About Me

~⁙⁙⁙~

"Letting go helps us to live in a more peaceful state of mind and helps restore our balance. It allows others to be responsible for themselves and for us to take our hands off situations that do not belong to us."

— Melodie Beattie

I felt betrayed. My friend took advantage of our friendship and of my generosity and I felt wounded. After all we've been through together. Any judge and jury would find her behavior irresponsible and would find her guilty as charged.

One day I realized how much energy it was taking to stay angry at my friend's behavior. She was nowhere near me, but my thoughts and energy were obsessed about her. It was as if she were standing next to me day and night. It was time to confront her and come to terms with her betrayal.

There was one sticking point. All my training over the years taught me that I am the only one responsible for my feelings. I can choose to feel betrayed, victimized, and angry. Or I can forgive her. Forgiveness did not seem like a possibility. But I knew I had to start somewhere.

When I was journaling one day I recalled a time when a coworker was angry at me and accused me of being disloyal to her and hurting her. It was never my intention. I had a lot of other things going on in my life at the time. It was never about her.

Is it possible it's not about me? No, not in this situation. This was too hurtful and purposeful. But what if it wasn't about me? All this anger and resentment would be an enormous waste of time and energy. Just thinking about it made me feel lighter. Maybe I could stop sending my friend mental daggers and send waves of peace instead.

It's worth a try. I'm willing to let go so I can find some peace. How about you?

AFFIRMATION: I choose to forgive. I choose to love.

Journal Practice

Make a list of people or situations you are willing to forgive.

Sounds of Silence

⟡⟡⟡

*"Silence is the great teacher and to learn
its lessons you must pay attention to it.
There is no substitute for the creative inspiration,
knowledge, and stability that come from knowing
how to contact your core of inner silence."*

— Deepak Chopra

I was in a meditation class in a busy downtown area. The window was open and I could hear the busy traffic. The instructor asked us to quiet our minds and all I could hear was the traffic noises. She said to find a place of peace and all I could hear was the traffic. It occurred to me that there is noise going on all the time in my mind—it wasn't just the traffic. In that moment, I was able to stop obsessing about the traffic and go within.

Until we give ourselves space to be quiet and listen to the sounds around us, we are caught up in someone else's ideas. It's wonderful to be able to relax with soothing music, be entertained or educated. But it is so important to take time to be in the silence. It gives us space to allow our own creativity to show up.

Take a few moments, close your eyes, and breathe. You may notice the noise around you but as you continue to breathe, your shoulders relax, your mind chatter lessens, and you are immersed in the silence.

Breathe. Release. Enjoy the sounds of silence.

AFFIRMATION: I relish my time in the silence.

Journal Practice

Put down your pen and breathe. Enjoy the sounds of silence.

Manifest Inner Peace

"When obstacles arise, you change your direction to reach your goal; you do not change your decision to get there."

— Zig Ziglar

Rude hotel staff, inadequate accommodations, tasteless food, and rainy weather were just a few things my friend shared about her less-than-perfect vacation. "Why did I create this?" she asked.

We often ask ourselves this misguided question. It's no wonder, since our world reminds us daily: Create your own reality, manifest your destiny, control your future. Those declarations sound great but stuff still happens. Challenges pop up. People don't keep their agreements. Yes, it even rains while you're on vacation.

When we look for someone to blame—or blame ourselves—we become the victim. We hang onto unwanted experiences and feel helpless to take action. I suggested to my friend that she ask a different question: "What did I learn from this experience?"

I reminded her that she successfully stepped out of her old pattern of suffering in silence. She spoke up and asked to be moved to another room. She reported the rude remarks from the hotel clerk to the manager. She left the resort and ate fabulous food at local restaurants. In spite of the rainy weather, she had a great vacation.

We create our reality, not by manipulating people and activities but by managing our response. We have the power to release attachment to the outcome and to choose to see things differently.

When we respond in love, it is easier to let go and remember that we have options. Our perception shifts. We move into compassion, patience, and inner peace—the one reality truly worth creating.

AFFIRMATION: I choose to react in peace and respond in love.

Journal Practice

Make a list of situations you are willing to see differently, without blame.

Are We There Yet?

~~~⟞⟝⟞⟝~~~

"Impatience is a failure to trust in the universal intelligence and it implies that we are separate from the all-providing spirit. Impatience implies that our ego is the boss of desire."

— Wayne Dyer

Have you noticed there is an impatient four-year-old who lives in your mind? Are we there yet? How much longer before we get there? How much time is this going to take?

Time takes forever when we are waiting for an event to happen but disappears when we are living in the moment. Time seems endless when we want our goal achieved but vanishes when we have released attachment to the results.

George Leonard shares in his book, *Mastery*, that in martial arts training, there is a moment when it appears the student is no longer improving.

The skill level seems stagnant and stuck. Actually on the inside there is an abundance of activity of the mind, body, and soul all coming into alignment. The challenge is not to stop practicing but to continue, regardless of the outside results. Progress is happening on an inner level that we can't see.

Change happens, not always on our time schedule. This is the practice of faith.

Faith isn't something we turn on or off. It is a seed planted in us. As we nurture and cultivate it, our faith grows deeper, stronger, and more profound.

Deepening faith doesn't happen overnight. It is a practice of monitoring our emotions and reprogramming old thoughts into new ones. We build faith when we find something to be grateful for in the midst of a challenge or experience, a moment of joy in the midst of sorrow.

Faith expands when we appreciate each day as a treasure and every experience as a gift. May your days be filled with patience, faith, and a sense of peace that you are doing exactly the right task, at the right time, with the perfect outcome.

AFFIRMATION: I have the faith to live each day with patience and peace.

Journal Practice

Make a list of events or activities you are willing to be patient with.

From the Inside Out

"We all have the extraordinary coded within us,
waiting to be released."

— Jean Houston

Promises to restore youthful appearance, energy, and vitality are abundant in our world today. Millions of dollars are spent on lotions, potions, and creams to slow down the aging process and keep us looking and feeling youthful.

If you've been on the spiritual journey for a while, you know the process works from the inside out. It's the clinging emotions on the inside that clogs our energy and vitality. Resentment, anger, victim-thinking sap our energy and keeps us tired and run down.

The cleansing process starts on the inside with forgiveness, self-love, and acceptance. Have you ever noticed that when a problem is solved or an issue resolved, you feel lighter, like a weight has been lifted off your shoulders? Freedom started on the inside. It changes how we carry ourselves and how we respond to others.

There is only one secret potion that will restore youth, vitality, and vigor. It is love. We already own it. Our work is to allow it to be revealed.

AFFIRMATION: I am whole, perfect, and complete, just as I am.

Journal Practice

Make a list of ways you are willing to express more self-love.

Avoid the Friends and Family Plan

~⟫⟫⟫~

"When you undervalue what you do, the world will undervalue who you are."

— Oprah Winfrey

Are you on the Friends and Family Plan? Not the one that gives free minutes on your phone, but the other one, the plan where you try to manage, fix, and organize the lives of your family, friends, and coworkers? After all, their problems are infinitely more interesting than yours. And they are so easy to fix, if they would only listen.

Helping others is admirable. It is also attractive because it takes attention away from our own challenges. But when we focus solely on solving someone else's problems, we take time and energy away from our own goals, dreams, and desires. We turn away from possibilities.

This is one of the strategies we use to avoid and procrastinate. It usually happens when we feel doubt about what we are doing. Even if we have ample experience and expertise, doubt stirs up a sense of fear—the fear of failure—that can keep us stuck. So we avoid it by helping others.

Taking one small step toward our own goals can begin to eliminate the feelings of doubt and fear. Every accomplishment, no matter how small, gives us encouragement to keep moving forward. Every step we take is helping us build faith.

Faith is an individual process of growth, patience, and willingness. It is up to us to let go of doubt and decide how we would like to express love in the world. Ultimately, love is our highest vision and faith is our guide. "Now faith is confidence in what we hope for and assurance about what we do not see." (*Hebrews 11:1*)

Faith is the freedom in knowing that whatever we need will be provided—whether it is strength to face the day, courage to speak our truth, or wisdom in when to help a loved one.

AFFIRMATION: I take affirmative action each day toward my goals.

Journal Practice

What doubts you are willing to release?

Practicing to Love My Neighbor

"A wise woman wishes to be no one's enemy; a wise woman refuses to be anyone's victim."

— Maya Angelou

Apples. It started with falling apples (inedible ones); hundreds of them from my neighbor's enormous, overgrown apple tree, falling into my flower bed and yard. How could my neighbors not be aware of this problem? Why would they not try to remedy the situation?

Turns out, they were away on vacation and oblivious to my distress. I became aware of my emotional reaction. I felt disrespected and ignored and perceived them to be my enemy.

Ah yes, perception. Perception is our awareness and discernment through our senses and our thinking. Our experiences, beliefs, culture, and history all influence our perception. While one person perceives a burning candle as peaceful and meditative, another approaches it with caution as a potential threat of fire.

I realized I was making up stories about why my neighbors were out to make my life miserable. STOP! The brain does not know the difference between what is imagined and what is real. I could feel my blood pressure rising and anxiety spiking. Over apples? Really?

I noticed I was not alone. I've heard stories from clients and friends about being left out of meetings, ignored at parties, and feeling abandoned by family members. It's so easy to fall into the trap of victim-thinking. If left unchecked, our perceptions will dictate whether we live in fear or faith.

It takes practice to reel in our emotions and choose again. There are so many solutions and options when we are not reacting to our emotions. Choosing peace instead of conflict can make a world of difference. And it can make a difference in our world.

I am choosing peace today. What about you?

AFFIRMATION: I look beyond the conditions in the world to see peace.

Journal Practice

What are the stories you are telling that keep you in victim-thinking?

The Reluctant Job Interview

⟨⟨⟨⟩⟩⟩

"Feel the fear. Have the doubts.
Go for it anyway."

— Barbara Stanny

There was a job opening at the nonprofit organization where I worked. The office administrator urged me to apply. What a waste of time and energy, I thought. They want a someone with a credential I don't have, four years of experience in a field in which I have none, and someone bilingual, which I am not. Did I really want to experience the rejection?

I reluctantly applied. The interview process consisted of a panel of eight people from the various agencies the position would partner with. It was an intense process during which each agency representative asked questions about my plans to meet their goals. I may not have had answers to every question, but I did understand what collaboration meant.

The day after the interview I was asked to schedule a second interview. I ran into the administrator who urged me to apply and asked how many others were asked back for a second interview. Just one, she said. I got the job—and it served me well for seven years.

I was afraid to take a risk. I didn't want to fail. How sad if I had missed the opportunity because of my own limiting thoughts.

If there is something you want to do, go do it. Take a chance. Risk being told no. Think outside the box.

AFFIRMATION: I can do this!

Journal Practice

Make a list of what you want to do. Visualize yourself doing it.

Mindful Possibilities

⌒⟋⟋⟍⟍⌒

*"Do not dwell in the past, do not dream of the future,
concentrate the mind on the present moment."*

— Buddha

Would you rather give yourself an electric shock than sit alone with your thoughts? If so, that's not as strange as you may think. A recent study at the University of Virginia found that 67 percent of men and 25 percent of women chose to give themselves a mild electric jolt rather than spend time alone with their thoughts.

It's easy to understand why. In our rare moments of silence, the inner critic uses the opportunity to criticize, chastise, and remind us of every failed endeavor and disappointing venture we've ever had. It's a wonder we get anything done at all.

Mindfulness is a technique that keeps us focused on the present. When practicing mindfulness, we become aware of our thoughts but resist the need to react to them. We don't give the inner critic the power to throw us off track. We notice our good behaviors and focus on the positive results in life.

Mindfulness allows us to be in the present and not rehash the past. When we live in the moment, we release attachment to our circumstances and experience freedom. Imagine all the time saved not being activated by what your coworker said or worried about what your friend thinks of you. When your mind is calm, you make room for creative ideas to bubble up as possibilities.

Practice mindfulness: stop, breathe, and release. When you find your emotions stirring and your mind reacting to circumstances, stop what you are doing, breathe deeply, and release the chatter of the inner critic.

Accept the moment of silence as a golden opportunity to receive all the good God has to offer.

AFFIRMATION: I joyfully live in the moment of now.

Journal Practice

What are you willing to do to be more mindful?

Choose Love

⁓⁕⁓

*"Let us always meet each other with a smile,
for the smile is the beginning of love."*

— Mother Teresa

What should have taken ten minutes to register online was now a three-hour phone call. A language barrier prevented the customer service agent from understanding my problem. My temper got the best of me, and I was short with her and irritated by our lack of communication. When I hung up, I felt frustrated and ashamed of my behavior. I seemed to have failed at my Christmas intention to speak with love.

I thought about it later. Would I have noticed my bad behavior if it was not the Christmas season? Or would I have just complained to my friends about this company's poor customer service?

During the Christmas season we go out of our way to show kindness toward strangers. We buy toys for children, donate canned goods to the food bank, contribute money and clothes to charities helping those in need. We buy gifts to show our friends and family that we love them.

But what happens on December 26? Does the Christmas spirit of kindness and compassion disappear? How do we keep it alive?

Whatever belief or faith you practice, there is one common denominator we share. Love. Love is the glue that holds us together and the elixir that soothes the frazzled life. Love unites us in time of crisis and heals when we feel the place of separation. Love is the place we go to forgive ourselves for our humanness and extend compassion for our inadequacies.

Love is a conscious awareness of our fragile existence here on Earth. Love is the awareness of seeing each other as our spiritual brothers and sisters, even when they don't behave in a way that we would approve. Love is the conscious awareness of the power of our thoughts and the significance of our words.

We can extend the season of love. We can decide if we will leave the heart open to the demands of love even after all the busy activities have subsided and the decorations put away. We can choose to set aside our human desires and turn within to listen to the whispers of what love has in store for us.

AFFIRMATION: I am open and receptive to all the blessings love has in store for me.

Journal Practice

Make a list of ways you are willing to practice random acts of kindness.

A Lifeline to Love

⁓᷍᷍⁓

"Fearlessness is not the absence of fear.
It's the mastery of fear.
It's about getting up one more time
than we fall down."

— Arianna Huffington

It seems like the world is adjusting to a new normal. We have been shaken, stirred, and left dizzy from the spinning changes to our jobs, homes, and sense of security. We helplessly watch the conflicts around the globe. When it feels like there is nothing left to hang onto, we can easily fall into fear.

There are those days when life feels fragile and fear invades my thoughts. Practicing gratitude is my lifeline out of the worry and doubt. I remember my loving friends and family who always show up when I need them the most. I give thanks for what I have rather than dwelling on what I don't have. I am grateful, knowing prayers are always answered, even if they don't fit my pictures at the time.

I am especially grateful to know that God's unconditional love is always present. I know that even in the midst of fear and doubt, my prayers are heard. From Isaiah 54:10: "'Though the mountains be shaken and the hills be removed, yet my unfailing love for you will not be shaken or my covenant of peace removed,' says the Lord, who has compassion for you."

I am grateful for you, for taking time from your busy day to read my thoughts. I pray, knowing you are abundantly blessed with God's gifts of love, joy, and peace.

AFFIRMATION: I am grateful for God's gracious Love.

Journal Practice

Make a list of current blessings in your life.

Once Upon a Time

⁓ ꙳꙳꙳ ꙳꙳꙳ ⁓

*"We cannot solve our problems
with the same thinking we used
when we created them."*

— Albert Einstein

My favorite childhood memory is of my dad reading bed-time stories to us. Whether he read them or made them up, they were uplifting and had a happy ending.

I realized recently that I make up stories all the time, usually in the middle of the night. My stories are not very uplifting—full of "what ifs" and "should haves." Rather than happy endings, they inflict enough emotional pain and suffering to cause any self-respecting insomniac to run for cover.

My greatest anxiety comes from my expectations about outcomes. Expectation comes from the mind and has me hoping and wishing that what I want will show up. The difference between expectation and expectancy is attachment. Expectancy comes from the soul and—rather than forming an attachment to the outcome—motivates me to look for the good in life.

Making up stories that create expectations leaves no place for God to show up. Most of my intuitive answers come out of the silence inherent in the question. If I can remember during stressful times, I write a question in my journal and resist the need to fill in the answer. There are many more possibilities to solve my problems than I can ever imagine. I have to be willing to sit in the silence and listen.

It comes down to having faith and trusting the process. Saying a prayer is far more productive than creating scary stories. God's abilities are far more inspiring than my worries.

Jesus looked at them and said, "With man this is impossible, but with God all things are possible." *(Matthew 19:26)*

AFFIRMATION: I see life through the eyes of love.

Journal Practice

What stories are you telling yourself? Are they fear-based or filled with possibilities?

A New Chapter

❧

*"You will learn a lot about yourself if you stretch
in the direction of goodness, of bigness,
of kindness, of forgiveness,
of emotional bravery. Be a warrior for love."*

— Cheryl Strayed

I remember the day I signed the closing papers on the sale of our home. It was so difficult to say goodbye to this beautiful home.

Our home served as a respite and sanctuary from the outside world for almost ten years. It was an environment for spiritual healing for clients and for students who attended classes. There were celebrations, birthday parties, dinners, and backyard barbecues. Our home served as a place of comfort while we grieved the loss of loved ones. It provided us a place of peace where my husband, Laurence, made his transition.

In my process of letting go, I realized the house did not make the memories. The house is simply the vessel for God's love to be revealed. The community of friends and family that gathered together is what made this house a home. I am grateful for all those who have blessed our home and created the rich experiences of life. I give thanks for the wisdom learned, love shared, and beauty expressed.

Truly nothing is lost in the process of letting go. I take with me all I experienced and learned. I am simply moving to a new chapter in the book of life.

I open my heart to the newness God has in store for me. I am so grateful for all that has been given and for so much more yet to come. I am grateful for friends and loved ones and for the opportunities to create new memories. I am grateful for all the ways God brings love into my life.

AFFIRMATION: I am grateful to open my heart to the new-ness God has in store for me.

Journal Practice

Make a list of things you are willing to let go of.

The Emotions of Money

⤙꙰⤚

"We come to recognize that God is unlimited in supply
and that everyone has equal access."

— Julia Cameron

For years I convinced myself that money was not important to me. I was a good girl and did not want people to
think I was greedy or selfish. So I limped along, trying to
make ends meet, hoping someday it would all work itself
out. That day came when my debt was too big to hide.

I decided to file bankruptcy and confessed everything to
my spiritual mentor. My relief in finally sharing my secret
quickly turned to shame and guilt for not paying attention
or taking action sooner.

Author Brené Brown says, "Shame is all about fear. When
we are experiencing shame, we are steeped in the fear of
being ridiculed, diminished, or seen as flawed." We want to
be loved and accepted and when we feel shame, we hide.
We can't possibly let others know how broken we are.

Money is a powerful reflection of our fears, emotions,
and beliefs. Suppressing and operating from fear is similar
to rearranging the deck chairs on the Titanic. Eventually,
that ship is going down.

For me, money was not the problem. Money was show-
ing me what I believed about life. It was time to change
my beliefs.

Rather than file bankruptcy, my mentor helped me create a plan for my finances. I took responsibility, talked to
my creditors, and set up a payment plan. I recorded my
expenses and was conscious of my spending.

I implemented spiritual practices and prayer in my life.
I explored my beliefs, forgave my mistakes, and developed
compassion for myself. I practiced gratitude, tithing, and
gave thanks for God's partnership in my life.

I clearly remember the day I wrote the last check. All my debts were paid in full. I was so grateful for all I learned along the way. I could not have walked it alone.

AFFIRMATION: I am open and receptive to all Spirit has in store for me.

Journal Practice

What beliefs do you have about money? What emotions are stirred up when you think of money?

Love While You Are Here

_"You don't get to choose how you're
going to die or when.
You can only decide how you are going to live. Now."_

— Joan Baez

When my husband, Laurence, was fighting cancer, I prayed he would outlive my parents. I couldn't imagine going through losing them without his strong shoulders to lean on. My mom made her transition sixteen months after Laurence left his earthly body. My experience of loss gave me the strength to be there for my dad, my sister, and my family members.

I spent many years thinking that if I prayed hard enough I could keep everyone I loved under God's umbrella of safety and they would be spared sickness and death. If I were good enough, perhaps the angel of death would just keep walking on by.

What I know now is that life is an extraordinary journey where we experience pain and joy, suffering and peace, loss and love. We will grieve those who leave us all too soon. We grieve because we love.

Our experience of life is sacred, amazing, crazy, and all too fleeting. Love guides us through life's challenges and nurtures us along the way.

Hug and kiss your loved ones. Call friends you haven't heard from. Forgive your enemies. Let go of old hurts. Life is so short. Love while you are here.

AFFIRMATION: I am grateful to be guided by love in all that I do.

Journal practice

What act of love can I offer today?

A Must-Have Chicken Soup Recipe

"I believe a joyful life is made up of ordinary moments, gracefully strung together by trust, gratitude, inspiration, and faith."

— Brené Brown

My mom made amazing chicken soup. My sister and I attempted to copy her recipe but our soup never tasted as delicious as hers. Something seemed to be missing. We jokingly accused Mom of leaving out the secret ingredient. She laughed and assured us we had all the information needed to make her soup.

Eventually, I realized there were two important ingredients that could not be duplicated. Mom had a passion for cooking and preparing food for others. Cooking was her gift to each of us. She prepared her meals with joy, knowing she would be sharing with family and watching everyone devour her scrumptious food.

Her recipe was quite simple: Passion + Joy = Love.

Isn't that really the recipe for life? Each of us is here to share our talents and gifts with each other. When we share our passions with joy, those receiving can't help but accept them with love. Love reflects back and is multiplied.

When I tried to copy Mom's soup recipe, I added extra spices, more vegetables, and tried cooking it longer, but still it did not taste the same. I was so attached to what I thought it should taste like that it became a chore and a struggle. I forgot to experience joy in my process.

I invite you to try this simple recipe when you celebrate with family and friends. Check your activities and make sure passion and joy are on your list. Let go of attachment to what you think the outcome should look like. Slow down, breathe deeply, and give thanks for all your blessings.

Remember that the ultimate aspiration is love.

AFFIRMATION: I experience a dose of joy in all my activities.

Journal Practice

Where attachments are you willing to let go of?

The Necessity of Faith

⌒⟶⟩⟩⟩⟩⟨⟨⟨⌒

"Nothing binds you except your thoughts;
nothing limits you except your fear;
nothing controls you except your beliefs."

— Marianne Williamson

In her book *Lean In: Women, Work, and the Will to Lead,* author Sheryl Sandberg shares that Forbes ranked her as the fifth most powerful woman in the world in 2011. Even though she was a CEO at Facebook, she felt embarrassed and self-conscious to be listed with such a powerful group of women. When anyone congratulated her, she told them the list was ridiculous.

Finally, her executive assistant took her aside and told her she was revealing her insecurity by not receiving the acknowledgement graciously. It was a wake-up call for Sandberg to recognize her doubts.

We all face doubts. Whether in the boardroom or on the assembly line, as a stay-at-home mom or an entrepreneur, we all have feelings of fear and misgiving. Doubt stops us from moving forward and using our talents and strengths to their full potential. Doubt weakens us and takes away our power—if we let it.

Here is the good news. Once we admit the doubt, we can begin to change it. We don't have to be victim to it. We can recognize our fears for what they are, get them under control, and take dominion over our own lives.

We can build our faith.

As we develop faith, we expand our awareness and realize we don't have to walk the path alone. A necessary step in our spiritual growth is to practice placing faith and trust in God. "Ask and it will be given to you; seek and you will find; knock and the door will be opened to you. For everyone who asks receives; he who seeks finds; and to him who knows, the door will be opened." *(Matthew 7:7-8)*

AFFIRMATION: I have faith that all I need is provided.

Journal Practice

What lingering doubts are you hanging onto?

Looking for Love in All the Wrong Places

〜〰〰〜

"Kindness in words creates confidence.
Kindness in thinking creates profoundness.
Kindness in giving creates love."

— Lao Tzu

Do you ever find yourself sitting alone, waiting to be recognized and acknowledged? Do you wish for someone to appreciate you just the way you are?

We all want to be loved and appreciated. The problem is we think it has to come from someone else. So we go looking for love in all the wrong places. We search for someone to validate the fact that we deserve to be loved. We hunt for someone to toss us a small morsel of appreciation.

Years ago I worked in an office and completed a difficult project in record time. My supervisor reviewed it, made some corrections, and shipped it off. After lunch she handed me the next project without a word of appreciation. I felt disappointed and neglected. I didn't know how to celebrate my accomplishment and give myself a pat on the back. I needed her approval. I resented her for the longest time.

The biggest obstacle that keeps us from love is hanging onto resentments from the past. It's like wanting to buy new shoes but the closet is full of old ones that are worn out or don't fit. There's no room for anything new.

And so it is with love. As we let go of old hurts and resentments we clear the way for love to come in.

Universal Law states that whatever we give out graciously comes back to us multiplied. If we want acknowledgment, we have to give it out. If we want to be appreciated, we have to show that appreciation to others. If we

want love, we find ways to extend love to those around us.
Here are three ways to get started:

- Catch yourself doing something right. Give yourself an "Attagirl! I knew you could do it."
- Practice random acts of kindness. The true gift is in the giving.
- Develop gratitude. Be grateful for all you have rather than counting what you don't have.

Love is an inside job. Loving ourselves gives us the ability to express appreciation and compassion for others. And yes, it does come back multiplied. Try it and see for yourself.

AFFIRMATION: I am willing to share my joy and love with others.

Journal Practice

List any resentments you are ready to let go of.

A Picture of Compassion

~~~)))))~~~

"The mind must reach a place where it no longer remembers the past with anxiety or looks to the future with uncertainty. It focuses instead on the divine goodness, the loving-kindness, and givingness of God."

— Ernest Holmes

I was so excited when my dad gave me my first camera and TWO rolls of film. It didn't take me long to find lots of wonderful subjects to photograph. They were mailed off to be developed, and I impatiently waited to see my work.

When the photos finally arrived, Dad opened the package and viewed my artistic expression. Why was he was frowning? I thought he would be pleased. Instead he scolded me. He reminded me that owning a camera is a responsibility and purchasing film and developing photos was expensive. Cameras were meant for taking pictures of people, not flowers, plants, and trees. He cautioned me to be more prudent with my picture taking.

Over the years of spiritual exploration, I've come to understand Dad's beliefs and behavior. He experienced poverty and hunger as a child. He left high school to help support his family. Making smart money decisions was an essential way of life.

I frequently meet people who live with the messages they were given years ago as children and their feelings of guilt and shame. They are sometimes resentful and blame past memories for keeping them from moving forward with their lives.

Often those messages were not meant to hurt us but to protect us and keep us from harm. When we are able to view the past with compassion and forgiveness, we change our experiences from fear-based to love.

Dad grew to love my photos. He looked forward to receiving them—especially the flowers—and was amazed at the photos taken with my smart phone.

I am grateful for his wisdom and all he taught me about money. I am grateful I was able to put his advice into perspective and understand his intention of love.

AFFIRMATION: I am grateful for the expressions of love that have supported me.

Journal Practice

Identify any past messages that no longer serve you.

It Only Takes a Moment

~∞∞∞~

"A single act of kindness throws out roots in all directions, and the roots spring up and make new trees. The greatest work that kindness does to others is that it makes them kind themselves."

— Amelia Earhart

My client, Monica, shared with me about her visit to a salon on her day off. The person scheduled to give her a pedicure was grumpy and out of sorts. Monica felt frustrated and resentful. She looked forward to this simple luxury, and now it was ruined by the very person who was supposed to pamper her.

Monica remembered that she had the power to change her experience. She silently began beaming love to the pedicurist. Soon the pedicurist began to share about her day and what was on her mind. Monica listened and continued to send her love. She later reported it was the best foot massage and pedicure she ever received.

We interact with dozens of people throughout our day, barely acknowledging their impact on our lives. Taking the time to appreciate and acknowledge others makes the world a better place. Compassionate listening, kind words, and loving thoughts are the simplest acts that have the greatest power to change our lives.

I invite you to experiment with practicing random acts of loving kindness. Find something uplifting to say to your coworker, spouse, or friend. Take a few moments to listen to someone who is having a difficult day. Send loving thoughts to the person who serves your coffee or is sitting in the car next to you at the red light.

A life overflowing with happiness can appear to be an elusive dream. It is not. It begins with the smallest drop of thoughtfulness and expands into a stream of love. Each act of loving kindness radiates out from us to be magnified and multiplied by Spirit, and we are all lifted up. The results are priceless.

AFFIRMATION: I send love and compassion to all those around me, seeing their spirits lifted up with joy.

Journal Practice

Recall a time when someone attentively listened to you or gave you a compliment on a bad day. How did it make you feel?

The Gift of Gratitude

꙰

*"If the only prayer you ever say in your entire life
is thank you, it will be enough."*

— Meister Eckhart

The hospital employee came in to empty the trash. "Thank you so much," Laurence said. "Where are you from?" "Guatemala," she replied. He asked her about her family, her life, and her journey to the United States.

My husband, Laurence, was in the hospital at the time, diagnosed with leukemia. It was just one more jolt in a long series of medical complications. Wherever he was or whatever he was doing, he always stopped to express his gratitude.

He said thank you to everyone. He thanked his business associates, children, family members, clients, and the clerk at the neighborhood deli. He thanked me for taking care of our home, for doing the laundry, and for buying the groceries. He said a prayer of thanks before every meal.

More trauma. A bone marrow transplant, complications with medications, a series of strokes. Laurence was in a coma for a week in intensive care. On day seven, his doctor told us to get his affairs in order.

Prayers intervened and Laurence miraculously awoke from his coma. As he regained consciousness, he began to whisper. Can you guess his first words? *Thank you.*

Laurence is no longer here on this earthly plane. But he left those of us who knew him with a reminder of the power of giving thanks. Gratitude acknowledges that we have received the gift that is being given, whether it is a compliment or an act of kindness. Gratitude puts us into a humbled state of appreciation. It connects us with God.

AFFIRMATION: I gratefully express my appreciation.

Journal Practice

Who are you grateful for?

A Journey of Love

"It is good to have an end to journey toward, but it is the journey that matters in the end."

— Ursula K. Le Guin

"How do you know if you have a fever?" That is the last question anyone ever wants to hear from a seatmate on a plane. I was on a twelve-hour flight from Rome to Los Angeles, returning from our ten-day pilgrimage in Italy. I was exhausted and sleep deprived and could not wait to close my eyes and get some sleep.

Now my adrenaline kicked in. I asked her if I could feel her forehead while I worked to calm the crazy chatter in my brain imagining all the worse-case scenarios of infectious disease on the plane. Yes, she most definitely had a fever. I gave her some water and shared my mini-pharmacy of essential oils, vitamins and herbal remedies. (OK, I confess: I am a health-obsessed Virgo and carry remedies wherever I go. For situations exactly like this one.)

I had chatted with this young woman earlier on the flight. She was traveling from Israel where she goes to school and was on her way to visit her parents in Los Angeles.

She finally settled down and went to sleep. I prayed and sent healing energy and light to her and to everyone on the plane. I finally got some sleep myself. By the time our flight landed, her color returned and she was feeling a little better.

A pilgrimage is a sacred journey we take to spend time in the presence of God. It was a blessing to be on this journey to visit the sacred sites in Rome, Assisi, Florence, and Venice. It was amazing to see the breathtaking art and beauty that has survived for centuries.

What made this pilgrimage so special to me was the

amazing group we traveled with, united with a common purpose to live as love. I observed our pilgrims caring for each other, sharing, supporting, and loving each other. We prayed for each other before and during our journey. Each person was a unique gift who reminded us of God's unlimited love.

My seatmate's question to me was a reminder to me that my pilgrimage was not over. The journey was not about finding God in a sacred church or basilica, but experiencing God's love in ordinary moments. Every moment is an opportunity to be in service and to love.

AFFIRMATION: My spiritual journey is one of service and love.

Journal Practice

How do you find God in ordinary moments?

Broken Open to Love

⚬ᔕᔕᕈᕈᕈᔕ⚬

"Love, and you shall be loved.
All love is mathematically just, as much as the
two sides of an algebraic equation."

— Ralph Waldo Emerson

After watching the outpouring of love that happens after mass shootings, I committed to being more loving toward others. I vowed to be more compassionate and more giving. I promised myself I would look for opportunities to serve others in need. My plan worked great ... for about three days.

On the return flight home from visiting a friend, I experienced airline delays, crying babies, and a bumpy ride. I arrived home to find unexpected home repairs and unfinished projects. My promise to be kinder and gentler now seemed like a distant memory. Where did I go wrong?

In times of sorrow and suffering, it is our human nature to reach out in love, and DO for others. In times of tragedy there is an outpouring of benevolence, compassion, and generosity. There are abundant accounts of people practicing random acts of kindness and giving graciously of their time, energy, and money.

Our spiritual nature is to BE the presence of love, every day.

When we make the commitment to live as love, we learn to listen when we disagree, help when we are too busy to stop, and forgive when others hurt us. Living as love compels us to step aside when the needs of others are greater than our own.

Love is a conscious awareness of our fragile existence here on Earth. We are aware of seeing each other as our spiritual brothers and sisters, even when they don't behave in a way that we would approve. We are aware of the power of our thoughts and the significance of our words.

We've been broken open. Now we must decide if we will leave the heart open to the demands of love even after all the busy activities subside. We must choose whether to set aside our human desires and turn within to listen to the whispers of what love has in store for us.

AFFIRMATION: I am willing to be a conscious presence of love.

Journal Practice

Where can you practice being more loving and compassionate?

Abundant Blessings

⤫⟨⟨⟩⟩⤫

*"The best and most beautiful things
in the world cannot be seen or touched...
but are felt in the heart."*

— Hellen Keller

I am often asked how we go about trusting God. Do we make our request and sit back and wait for God to deliver? Or do we stay busy doing what we are doing and hope for the best? How do we know what to do?

Faith is a balance of reflection and action. Meditation, mindfulness, and prayer are ways to maintain our God connection. Through prayer we recognize our oneness with God and acknowledge our good. Observing the awesome beauty of nature reminds us of our abundance. When we say grace before a meal, we are appreciating our blessings.

When we have a goal or intention, it's up to us to follow through on the steps needed to achieve results. At the same time, we give thanks for the opportunity to share our gifts. Sometimes it's a challenge to resist judging our circumstances. Giving thanks helps to quiet the chatter of the inner critic.

It takes but a moment to stop in the midst of our busy day and gaze at the wonder around us and feel gratitude. Life's activities will still be there when we return.

As we pause and give thanks for the awesomeness of God, we open our heart and mind to all the good available to us. The attitude of gratitude unites us with the desires of the heart. Gratitude is not a technique to get rich but a rich way of thinking that opens us to abundance.

AFFIRMATION: I am grateful for the beauty and wonders that surround me.

Journal Practice

Make a list of all the things you are grateful for.

Heart Opening

*"Prayer is simply talking to God like a friend
and should be the easiest thing we do each day."*

— Joyce Meyer

Is your soul weary? We are living in a world of high drama with not a moment to rest before the next adrenaline-pumping news story makes its way to our attention.

I have heard a comment over the past few weeks that prayer is not enough to deal with the changes in the world; we need to take action. I agree! And prayer can be the catalyst and the inspiration to take action.

When I was growing up, I believed I was powerless and my prayer was needed to make sure God would hear my plea for resources, funds, and opportunities. I prayed for a miracle, thinking it was something God did alone.

Now I know that prayer is a practice that comes not out of neediness but out of power. I recognize the Creative Power of all life that is God, and I am one with all God is. I am expectant and receptive. My energy is raised to one of love, peace, and harmony—and my mind is now open to limitless potential.

Prayer is my foundation, a stepping-off place where I take action in love instead of anger and in peace instead of resentment. My heart opens to love, gratitude, and compassion.

This is not just a hopeful theory. In his book *Soul Awakening,* James O'Dea shares, "Science confirms the practice of building deep heart coherence through love and gratitude. When we feel compassion, the body's electrical and biochemical systems radiate peace and wellness."

Prayer is heart opening, life affirming, wisdom creating, and love activating. Together we can raise the vibration of love.

Thank you for praying. Your prayer makes a difference. Your prayer move us into greater love.

And the world is ready for your infusion of love.

AFFIRMATION: I am expectant and receptive and live in love.

Journal Practice

Create a list of what you want to pray for.

God Is Always Present

*"When you love you should not say,
'God is in my heart,' but rather, 'I am in the heart
of God.' And think not you can direct the
course of love, for love, if it finds you worthy,
directs your course."*

— Kahil Gibran

As a child in Catholic school, I often imagined the opulence and mystery of heaven. It seemed to be a magical place where there was peace, love, and all the ice cream I could eat. However, there seemed to be a lot of stuff to do (or not do) before I could be good enough to live there.

Today I understand that the blessings of heaven are available to me now. When I align myself with spiritual principles to find peace of mind, it feels heavenly. I experience serenity when I live in the consciousness awareness of God's love.

The presence of God is not limited to a church, a mosque, or a temple. God is found in our struggles and successes, in good days and bad.

We can have a mental understanding of what we think God is. But when we practice mindfulness in our day-to-day moments, we become aware of our powerful connection with God's unfailing love.

Every opportunity is a chance to connect with God. In quiet moments, in simple reflections, or chance opportunities we are awakened to the fact that God is ever present.

AFFIRMATION: I am open and receptive to receiving God's unfailing love.

Journal Practice

What do you believe about God and heaven?

Gut Punched

"Tears are the silent language of grief."

— Voltaire

I remember standing in the parking lot/playground at my Catholic elementary school, talking with my friends. Suddenly a younger boy came out of nowhere, ran up to me and punched me in the stomach.

The punch did not hurt as much as much as the shock of the unexpected. The overwhelming emotion from being attacked. Of being violated. I had no idea why I was his target.

Watching the floods in Houston was heartbreaking. But watching the news video of the flames burning in the Columbia River Gorge in Oregon ripped open a hole in my soul. A fathomless wound. A punch in the gut. I know I was not alone.

I realized that the Columbia River Gorge is not just a place, it is an experience. It is a presence. The gorge exemplifies all that God is—beauty, peace, harmony, abundance, opulence, freedom, joy, unity. When I am in the Columbia River Gorge, my soul is fed, my heart is nurtured. I love hiking in the peaceful forest, dipping my toes in an ice cold stream, and feeling the spray of a waterfall on my face. I relish the smell of the trees, hearing the wind rustling the branches, and seeing miles of beauty wherever I look.

I grieve for what was. I mourn for all those who have lost their homes and livelihoods. I pray for safety for all the firefighters and the families still in harm's way. I pray for rain. And for the flames to stop. Just please stop.

I invite you to join me in sending love to any place that you mourn or may have lost. The presence is not gone. The Creative Process that is God will resurrect, renew, and replenish.

In the meantime, we grieve together.

AFFIRMATION: I see the presence of God in all places.

Journal Practice

What things bring you joy? What experiences cause you to feel the presence of God around you?

What I Know for Sure

~sɔɔ)ɔɔ~

"Everything is really full of love for you.
The good that is for you loves you as much as
you love it. The good that is for you seeks
you and will come flying to you
if you see that what you love is love itself."

— Emma Curtis Hopkins

I know life is amazing and can also be terrifying. I know life is abundant and often there is scarcity. I know there is kindness and goodness and yet there also is hatred and resentment.

I know most of the time life doesn't seem to make sense and the problems of the world appear to be incredibly overwhelming.

Yet, what I know for sure is that there is a power for good, a source of creativity and peace and joy. Whatever you may call this presence, I know it as love. I know love is unconditional, everlasting, and ever present—even in the midst of confusion, sorrow, and pain.

I know love is everywhere and in everyone and that I am willing to see beyond the contradictions of the world to see love in every person. I am willing to see beyond confusion to know the presence of love is at the center of every activity.

What I know for sure is that you and I are on this amazing journey to know and see love for each other and ourselves.

I know that even in the midst of fear and doubt, our prayers are always answered.

I know you are abundantly blessed with God's gifts of love, joy, and peace.

AFFIRMATION: I know the presence of love is at the center of every activity.

Journal Practice

What do you know for sure?

In Gratitude

⟿⟿⟿

I am truly grateful to all those who edited my drafts, listened to my ideas, and encouraged my writing over the years. My heart was inspired every time someone said, "I loved what you wrote."

This book lived in my computer patiently waiting for me to bring it to life. Divine timing brought editor Julie Mierau and book designer Maria Robinson of Designs on You, LLC, together to work their artistic magic. I am so grateful for their creative talent and passion.

I acknowledge my friends, family, clients, and students who served as my inspiration. I would not be the spiritual teacher I am today without you in my life.

I appreciate you for purchasing and reading my books. I am grateful to serve you on your spiritual journey.

Christine

About The Author

Christine Green finds her inspiration in empowering others to grow beyond their limitations and discover their inner strength and courage. She is an author, facilitator, speaker, and minister and has a background in business and education and a master's degree in Religious Studies.

Christine finds joy in offering seminars, workshops, and retreats, providing participants with tools and practices to expand their awareness and to overcome life's obstacles. She lives in Lake Oswego, Oregon, and enjoys hiking, travel, photography, and cleaning out closets. Learn more at www.revchristine.com.

Made in United States
Troutdale, OR
12/10/2023

15637627R00076